UNDERSTAND YOUR Mind AND Body

Hearing Loss

AJ Knight

Explore other books at:
WWW.ENGAGEBOOKS.COM

VANCOUVER, B.C.

e→ WWW.ENGAGEBOOKS.COM

Hearing Loss: Understand Your Mind and Body
Knight, AJ
Text © 2023 Engage Books
Design © 2023 Engage Books

Edited by: A.R. Roumanis Ashley Lee,
Melody Sun, and Sarah Harvey
Design by: Mandy Christiansen

Text set in Montserrat Regular.
Chapter headings set in Hobgoblin.

FIRST EDITION / FIRST PRINTING

This book is not meant to replace the advice of a medical professional or be a tool for diagnosis. It is an educational tool to help children understand what they or other people are going through.

LIBRARY AND ARCHIVES CANADA CATALOGUING IN PUBLICATION

Title: Hearing loss / AJ Knight.
Names: Knight, AJ, author.
Description: Series statement: Understand your mind and body

Identifiers: Canadiana (print) 20230447015 | Canadiana (ebook) 20230447023
ISBN 978-1-77878-169-8 (hardcover)
ISBN 978-1-77878-170-4 (softcover)
ISBN 978-1-77878-171-1 (epub)
ISBN 978-1-77878 172-8 (pdf)
ISBN 978-1-77878-112-4 (audio)

Subjects:
LCSH: Deafness in children—Juvenile literature.
LCSH: Deafness—Juvenile literature.
LCSH: Deafness—Prevention—Juvenile literature.
LCSH: Deafness—Treatment—Juvenile literature.

Classification: LCC RF291.5.C45 K65 2023 | DDC J618.92/0978—DC23

This project has been made possible in part by the Government of Canada.

Canada 🍁

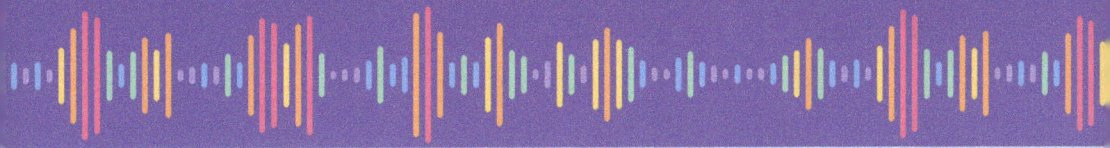

Contents

4   What Is Hearing Loss?

6   What Causes Hearing Loss?

8   How Does Hearing Loss Affect Your Brain?

10 How Does Hearing Loss Affect Your Body?

12 What Is It Like to Have Hearing Loss?

14 Can Hearing Loss Go Away?

16 Asking for Help

18 How to Help Others With Hearing Loss

20 The History of Hearing Loss

22 Hearing Loss Superheroes

24 Hearing Loss Tip 1: Protecting Your Ears

26 Hearing Loss Tip 2: Adapting Your Life

28 Hearing Loss Tip 3: Connecting With Others

30 Quiz

What Is Hearing Loss?

People with hearing loss cannot hear as well as other people. Someone can have hearing loss in one or both ears. Some people only lose a small part of their hearing. Others lose a lot.

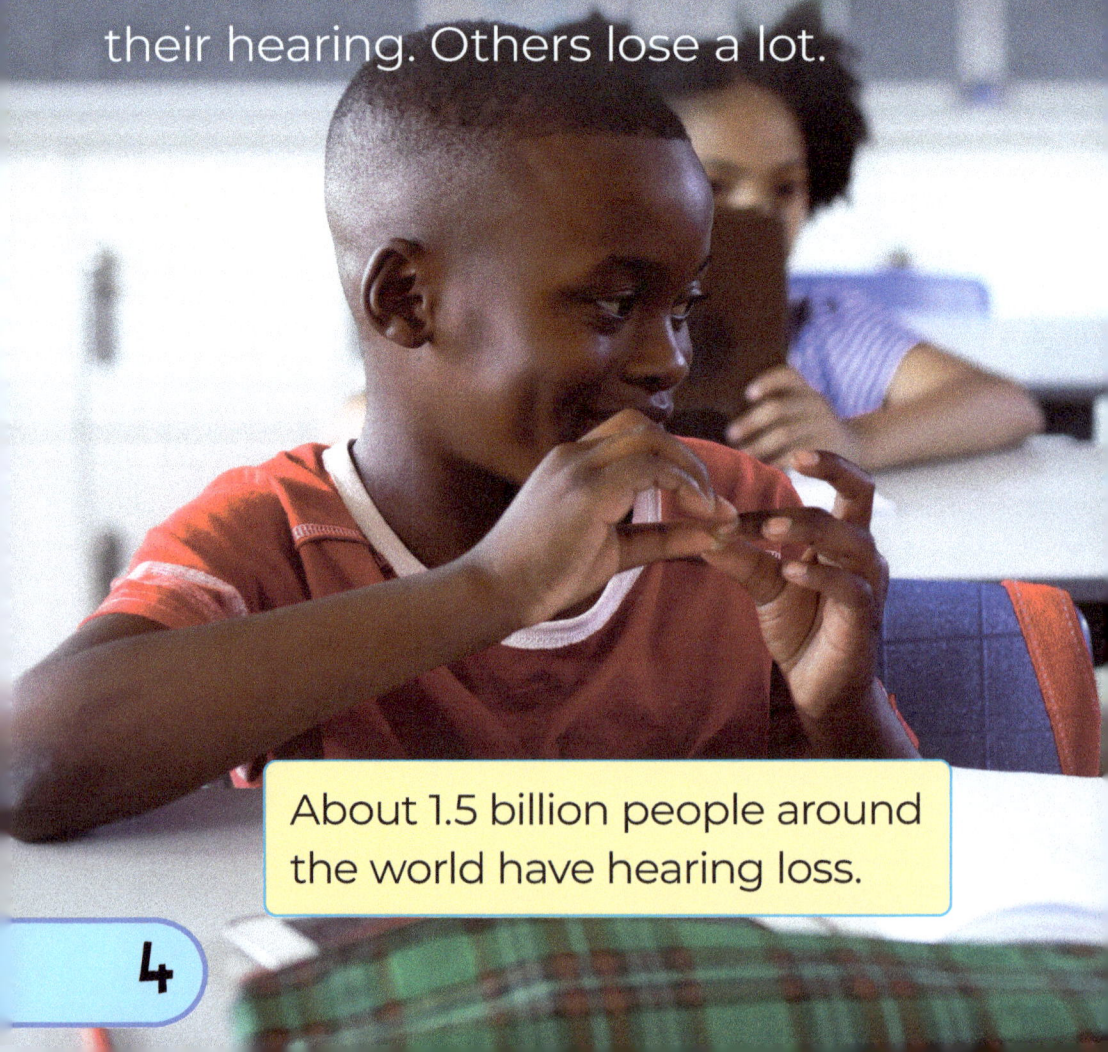

About 1.5 billion people around the world have hearing loss.

People with hearing loss may **identify** as Deaf. The Deaf community is a group of people who share the experience of having hearing loss. There are many different ways to be Deaf, and they are all okay.

KEY WORD

Identify: when someone sees themselves as belonging to a certain group.

What Causes Hearing Loss?

There are many reasons someone may have hearing loss. Some people are born with hearing loss while others get it later. Sometimes hearing loss runs in families.

About 90 percent of children born with hearing loss are born to hearing parents.

One of the most common causes of hearing loss is loud noise. It can also be caused by some illnesses. Many people get hearing loss as they get older.

How Does Hearing Loss Affect Your Brain?

The **auditory cortex** is the part of the brain that helps people understand sound. It can change in people with hearing loss to help them understand **vibrations** better. This allows them to enjoy music by feeling the musical vibrations.

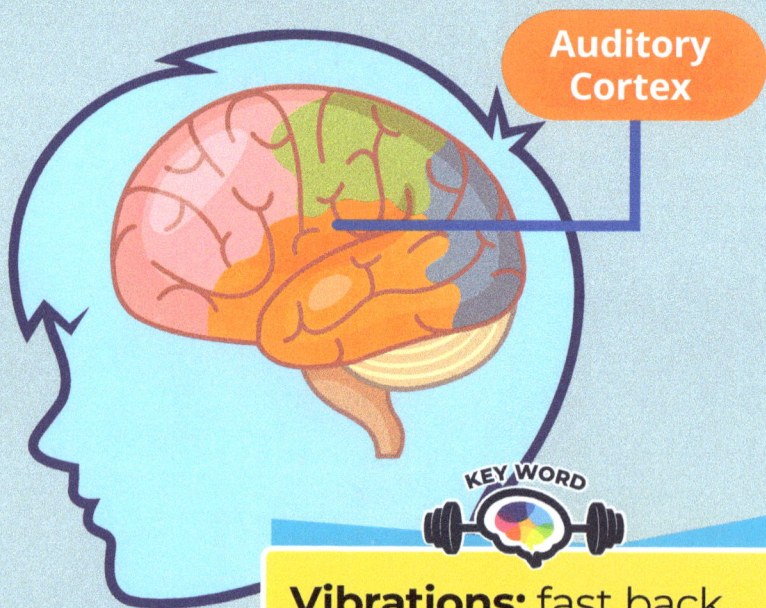

Auditory Cortex

KEY WORD

Vibrations: fast back and forth movements.

A person's mental health can be affected when they first learn they have hearing loss. They may feel sad, worried, or **stressed**. It may take some time for these feelings to go away.

KEY WORD

Stressed: when people feel uncomfortable about something that is happening.

How Does Hearing Loss Affect Your Body?

The ear has three main parts. These are the inner ear, the middle ear, and the outer ear. All three parts help people hear.

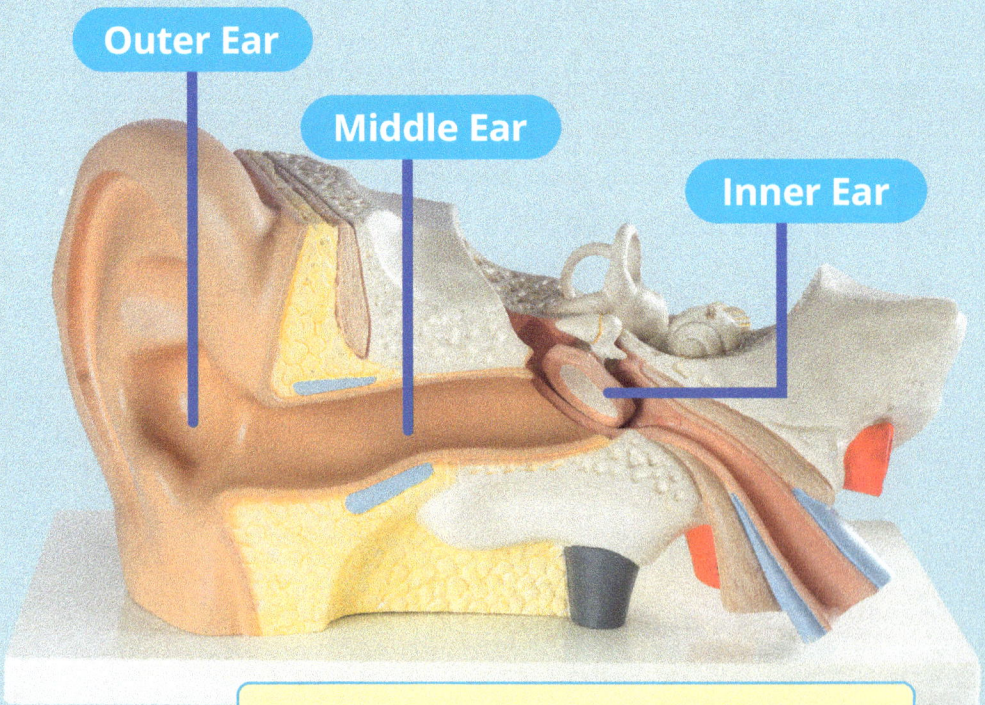

Outer Ear

Middle Ear

Inner Ear

The inner ear is the part of the ear affected by loud noises.

Hearing loss can affect any of these parts. It can also affect more than one part of the ear. Hearing loss that affects the inner ear and the middle or outer ear is called mixed hearing loss.

What Is It Like to Have Hearing Loss?

People with hearing loss might have a hard time hearing in loud places or when people are talking at the same time. They also might have trouble finding where a sound is coming from.

Some people with hearing loss may use devices to help them hear better. Hearing aids make sounds louder and are worn behind the ear. Cochlear implants are placed in the inner ear with surgery. They help people understand certain sounds better.

Cochlear implants come in lots of different colors.

Can Hearing Loss Go Away?

Some types of hearing loss can go away. **Temporary** hearing loss can be caused by loud noises or too much earwax. A doctor can find the cause and give the person medical care.

KEY WORD

Temporary: lasting a short amount of time.

Temporary hearing loss from loud noises will often get better by going to a quiet place.

Some hearing loss does not go away. This is okay. People with hearing loss can still live full lives.

Asking for Help

Talk to an adult if you notice changes to your hearing. An adult can help you figure out why your hearing has changed and if you should see a doctor. A doctor may be able to fix the cause or give you devices to make your hearing better.

"I have trouble hearing my teacher during class. Can we get my ears checked?"

"My ears have been ringing all day. Do you know why?"

"My left ear hurts and it's hard to hear out of. Can we go to the doctor?"

How to Help Others With Hearing Loss

When people talk to each other, they all have to do their best to make the conversation work. When talking to someone with hearing loss, there are some things you can do to make sure you are communicating well.

Speak normally

Speak louder or more slowly only if someone asks you to. Do not assume you need to yell when talking to someone with hearing loss.

Speak one at a time

Take turns speaking. Try not to speak when someone else is talking. This will make it easier for everyone to understand the conversation.

Learn a sign language

Sign languages are languages where people talk using their hands rather than their mouths. There are many different sign languages. Look online to find out which one people in your area use.

The History of Hearing Loss

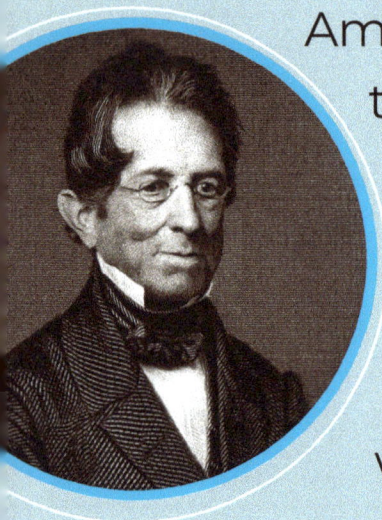

Thomas Hopkins Gallaudet created American Sign Language in the early 1800s. He wanted to help his neighbor's Deaf daughter. He opened America's first school for the Deaf in 1817 with a French Deaf man named Laurent Clerc.

In the 1800s, ear trumpets were popular for people with hearing loss. The small end of a horn would go in the ear and the large end would stick out. The horn would collect sound for people to hear.

Miller Reece Hutchison was on a boat with a friend when he noticed his friend could not hear the boat's whistle. Miller wanted to help his friend so he began studying hearing at school. He invented the first electronic hearing aids in 1898.

Hearing Loss Superheroes

People with hearing loss can sometimes feel like they are alone. But there are many people around the world who have it as well. Here are some superheroes who are helping people with hearing loss.

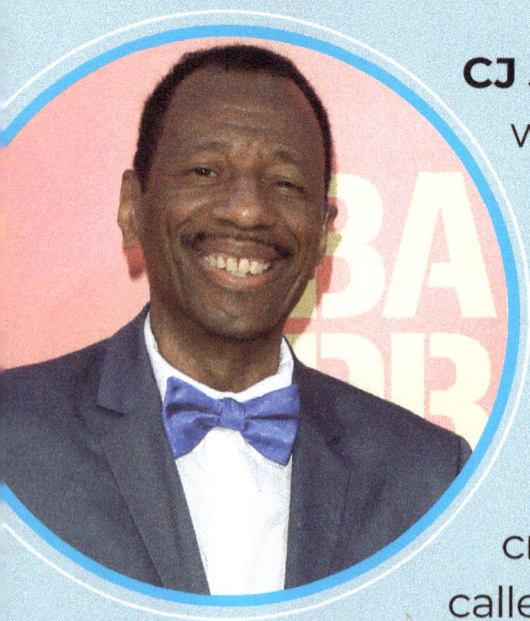

CJ Jones is an actor who lost his hearing at age seven after becoming sick. CJ has worked hard to make sure people with hearing loss feel accepted. He created a TV show called *Once Upon a Sign* that tells fairy tales using sign language.

Chella Man is a deaf artist. He first got cochlear implants at 12 after slowly losing his hearing. Chella uses his **social media** to teach people about hearing loss.

KEY WORD

Social media: websites like Instagram that allow people to connect with others.

Millicent Simmonds is an actress who lost her hearing as a child. Her mom learned sign language and taught it to Millicent. Millicent now helps raise awareness about the Deaf community.

Hearing Loss Tip 1: Protecting Your Ears

Hearing loss can get worse if you are not careful. But there are simple things you can do to protect your hearing. Turn the volume down when wearing headphones. Try to stay away from loud noises.

If you are going to be around loud noises, wear something to protect your ears. Noise-canceling headphones look just like normal headphones, but they help block out sound. Earplugs are made of a soft material and are placed inside the ear. They also help block out sound.

Hearing Loss tip 2: Adapting Your Life

Adapting means changing something to fit a new situation or to make things better. You can adapt to hearing loss by using extra supports. Supports are things that help you.

1. Use a doorbell that lights up instead of rings.

2. Use an alarm clock that vibrates.

3. Turn on captions for movies and TV.

4. Use a **sign language interpreter**.

KEY WORD

Sign language interpreter: someone who can help people who use sign language communicate with people who do not know sign language.

Hearing Loss Tip 3: Connecting With Others

Having friends is nice for anyone. But connecting with others like you can help you feel like part of the Deaf community. Connect with the Deaf community in your area or ask an adult for help connecting online.

The Deaf community has its own **culture**. The community and its culture help people feel like they belong. They help people feel good about who they are.

KEY WORD

Culture: the values, beliefs, and behaviors of a group of people.

Quiz

Test your knowledge of hearing loss by answering the following questions. The questions are based on what you have read in this book. The answers are listed on the bottom of the next page.

1 How many people around the world have hearing loss?

2 What is one of the most common causes of hearing loss?

3 What are the three main parts of the ear?

4 What are sign languages?

5 What should you do if you are going to be around loud noises?

6 What is culture?

Explore Other Level 3 Readers.

ENGAGING READERS — LEVEL 3
ADHD
AJ Knight

ENGAGING READERS — LEVEL 3
Anxiety
Adelaide Wilder

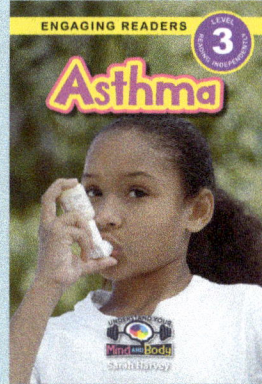
ENGAGING READERS — LEVEL 3
Asthma
Sarah Harvey

ENGAGING READERS — LEVEL 3
Body Image
Adelaide Wilder

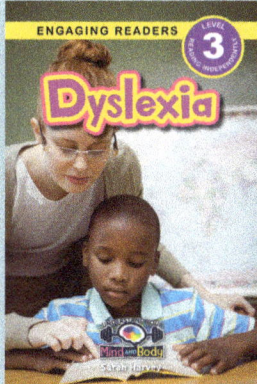
ENGAGING READERS — LEVEL 3
Dyslexia
Sarah Harvey

ENGAGING READERS — LEVEL 3
Diabetes
Kit Caudron-Robinson

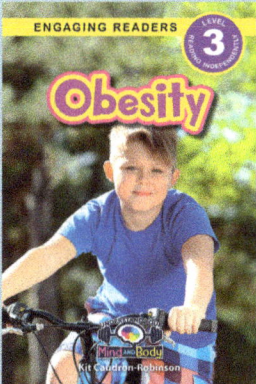
ENGAGING READERS — LEVEL 3
Obesity
Kit Caudron-Robinson

ENGAGING READERS — LEVEL 3
Speech Disorders
AJ Knight

ENGAGING READERS — LEVEL 3
Vision Loss
Hannalora Leavitt & Sarah Harvey

Visit www.engagebooks.com/readers

Answers:
1. About 1.5 billion 2. Loud noise 3. The inner ear, the middle ear, and the outer ear. 4. Languages where people talk using their hands rather than their mouths 5. Wear something to protect your ears 6. The values, beliefs, and behaviors of a group of people

www.ingramcontent.com/pod-product-compliance
Lightning Source LLC
Chambersburg PA
CBHW040227040426
42331CB00039B/3409